Teaching Little Fingers to Play Classics

11 Piano Solos with Optional Teacher Accompaniments

Arranged by Randall Hartsell

CONTENTS

Cover Design by Nick Gressle

ISBN 978-1-4234-0884-0

EXCLUSIVELY DISTRIBUTED BY

HAL•LEONARD®

7777 W. BLUEMOUND RD. P.O. BOX 13819 MILWAUKEE, WI 53213

WILLIS MUSIC

Visit Hal Leonard Online at
www.halleonard.com

Rests

In music notation there are SIGNS of SILENCE, called RESTS, which tell us when and for how long our fingers should be silent.

QUARTER REST 𝄽 = 1 count

WHOLE REST* 𝄻 = 4 counts in this piece!

*The WHOLE REST receives the counts for the whole measure indicated by the top number of the time signature.

Eighth Notes

The time value of an eighth note ♪ is HALF as long as that of a quarter note. Play TWO eighth notes to one count.

Student Position

One Octave Higher When Performing as a Duet

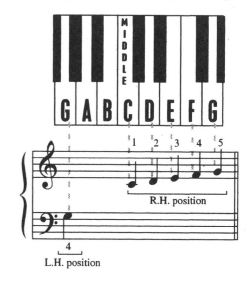

Ode to Joy
(from Symphony No. 9)

Optional Teacher Accompaniment

Ludwig van Beethoven
Arr. Randall Hartsell

Ode to Joy

(from Symphony No. 9)

Play both hands one octave higher when performing as a duet.

Ludwig van Beethoven
Arr. Randall Hartsell

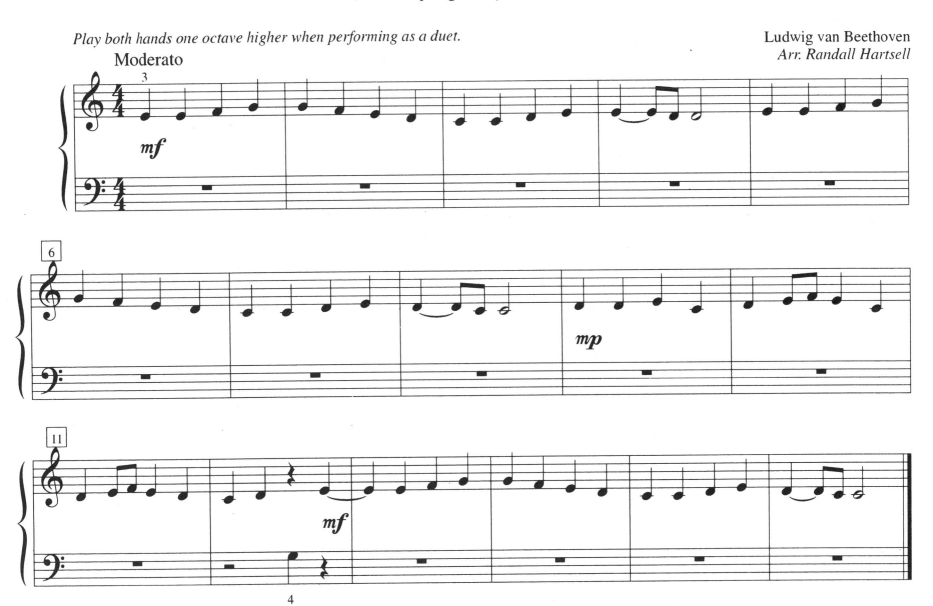

4

The Dotted Half Note ♩.
(THREE-BEAT NOTE)
HOLD FOR 3 BEATS (1, 2, 3)
A DOT after a note increases
the value of that note by one half.

Dynamics
DYNAMICS are suggestions by the
composer to help create contrasts in
your music. Watch for the *loud* ($\boldsymbol{f}$)
in this piece.

Student Position
One Octave Higher When Performing as a Duet

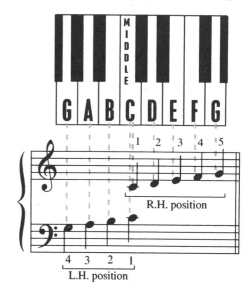

A Little Night Music
(from *Eine kleine Nachtmusik*)

Optional Teacher Accompaniment

Wolfgang Amadeus Mozart
Arr. Randall Hartsell

A Little Night Music

(from *Eine kleine Nachtmusik*)

Play both hands one octave higher when performing as a duet.

Wolfgang Amadeus Mozart
Arr. Randall Hartsell

Staccato

When a note has a dot under or over it, play the key like it's "hot"! The Italian word for this is STACCATO and it means to play crisply and detached.

Accidentals

A SHARP or FLAT placed next to a note but not found in the key signature is called an ACCIDENTAL and only changes the pitch for the measure in which it occurs.

Student Position

One Octave Higher When Performing as a Duet

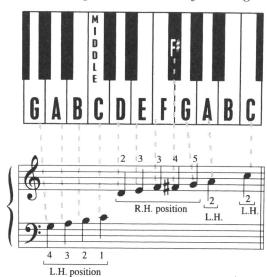

"Surprise" Symphony

Optional Teacher Accompaniment

Joseph Haydn
Arr. Randall Hartsell

"Surprise" Symphony

Play both hands one octave higher when performing as a duet.

Joseph Haydn

Arr. Randall Hartsell

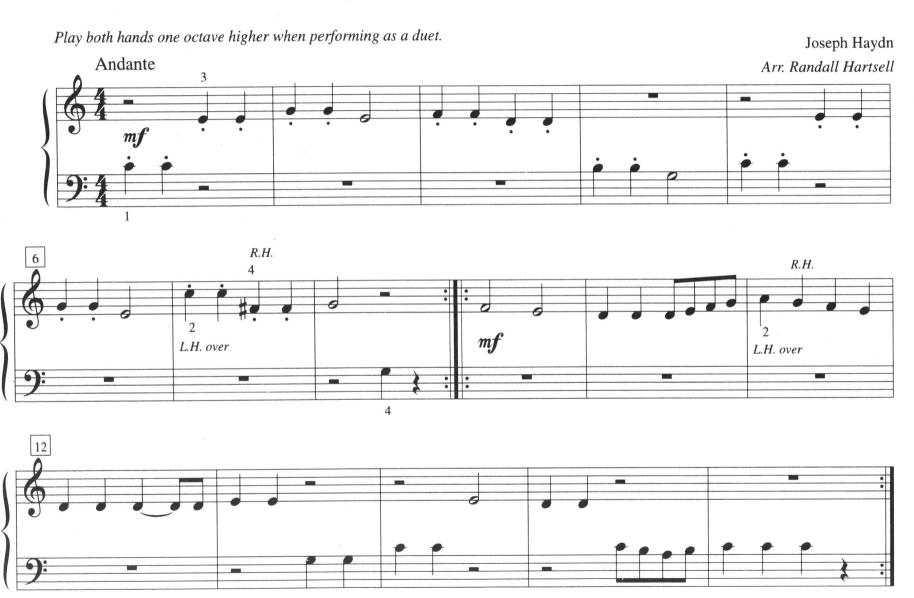

Crescendo - Decrescendo

When you see these

gradually get louder then gradually get softer.

Student Position
One Octave Higher When Performing as a Duet

Bridal Chorus
(from *Lohengrin*)

Optional Teacher Accompaniment

Richard Wagner
Arr. Randall Hartsell

Bridal Chorus

(from *Lohengrin*)

Play both hands one octave higher when performing as a duet.

Richard Wagner
Arr. Randall Hartsell

The Tie

The TIE is a curved line joining one note to another of the SAME PITCH. Play the first note and hold for the value of both.

Student Position
One Octave Higher When Performing as a Duet

Symphony No. 5
(Second Movement)

Optional Teacher Accompaniment

Peter Ilyich Tchaikovsky
Arr. Randall Hartsell

Symphony No. 5
(Second Movement)

Play both hands one octave higher when performing as a duet.

Peter Ilyich Tchaikovsky
Arr. Randall Hartsell

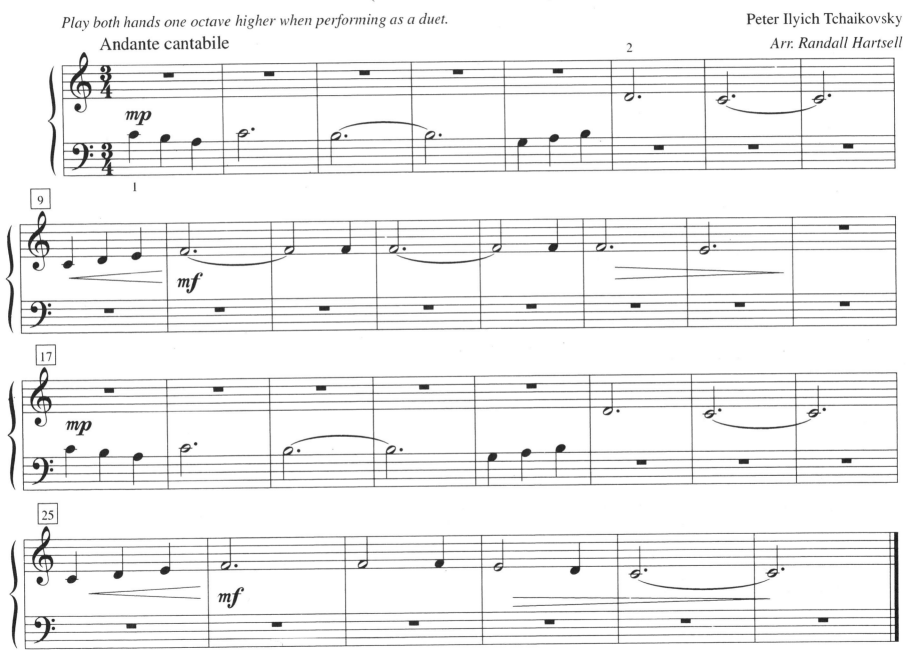

12

> ## Ritardando
> This means to gradually slow down.

Student Position
One Octave Higher When Performing as a Duet

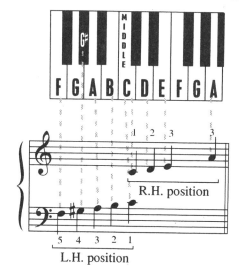

Swan Lake

Optional Teacher Accompaniment

Peter Ilyich Tchaikovsky
Arr. Randall Hartsell

Swan Lake

Play both hands one octave higher when performing as a duet.

Peter Ilyich Tchaikovsky

Arr. Randall Hartsell

Student Position
One Octave Higher When Performing as a Duet

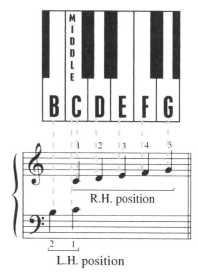

Patterns
Groups of notes that are repeated in a PATTERN can help you to memorize your piece. Practice the patterns first, then put it all together.

Barcarolle
(from *Tales of Hoffman*)

Optional Teacher Accompaniment

Jacques Offenbach
Arr. Randall Hartsell

Barcarolle
(from the Opera *Tales of Hoffman*)

Jacques Offenbach
Arr. Randall Hartsell

Play both hands one octave higher when performing as a duet.

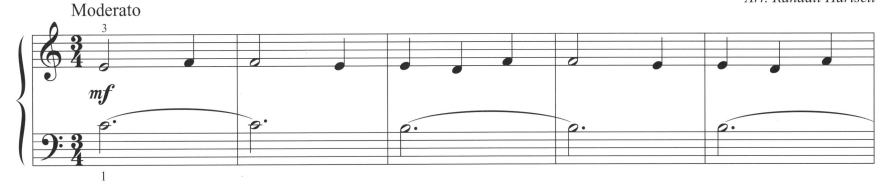

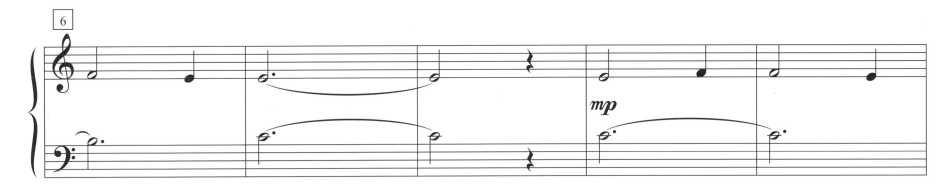

Key Signature

When the SHARP sign (♯) is placed between the clef sign and the time signature it becomes the KEY SIGNATURE. In this piece all F's must be sharped. (Play the first black key to the right of F.)

Student Position

One Octave Higher When Performing as a Duet

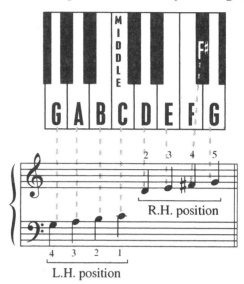

Can-Can
(from *Orpheus in the Underworld*)

Optional Teacher Accompaniment

Jacques Offenbach
Arr. Randall Hartsell

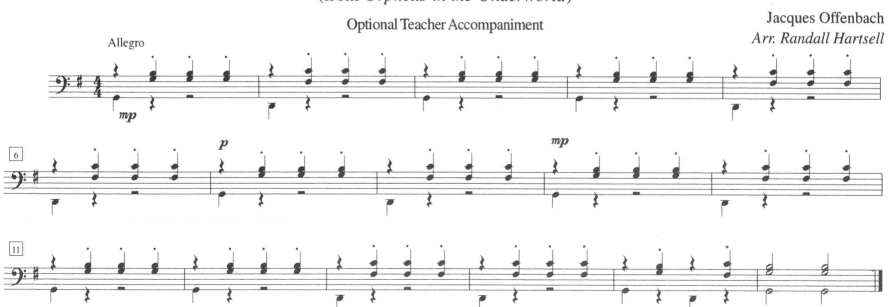

Can-Can

(from *Orpheus in the Underworld*)

Jaques Offenbach
Arr. Randall Hartsell

Play both hands one octave higher when performing as a duet.

An Incomplete Measure

This piece begins on beat THREE.
You must accent the first beat AFTER
the bar line.

Key Signature

When the FLAT sign (♭) is placed between the clef
sign and the time signature it becomes the KEY
SIGNATURE. In this piece all B's must be flatted.
(Play the first black key to the left of B.)

Student Position

One Octave Higher When Performing as a Duet

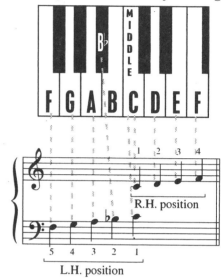

Lullaby

Optional Teacher Accompaniment

Johannes Brahms
Arr. Randall Hartsell

Lullaby

Play both hands one octave higher when performing as a duet.

Johannes Brahms
Arr. Randall Hartsell

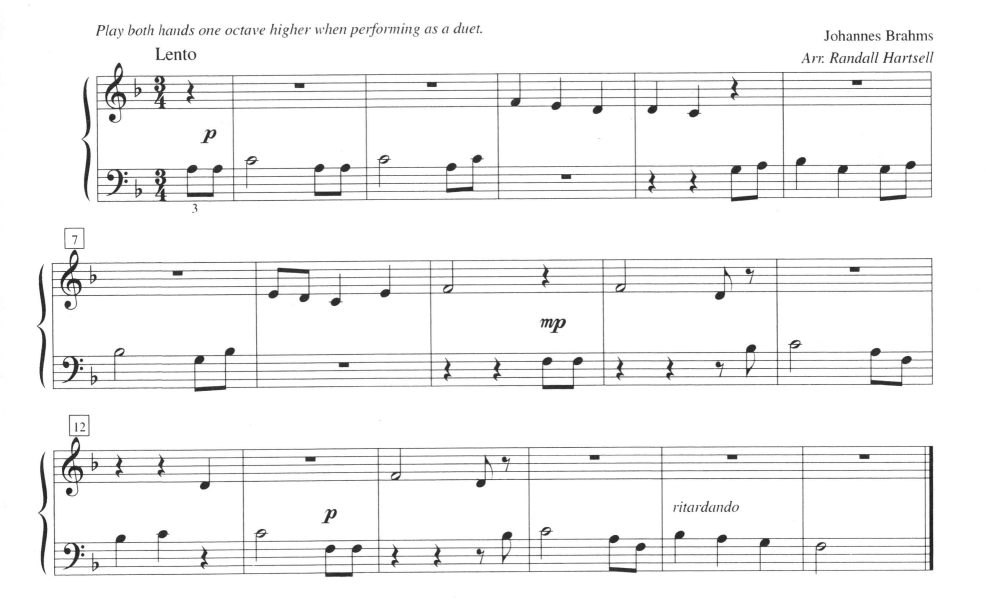

Student Position
One Octave Higher When Performing as a Duet

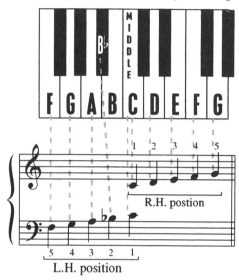

The Phrase
Groups of notes, like words in books, tell stories when they are arranged in 'sentences' and punctuated. A curved line over a group of notes indicates a MUSICAL SENTENCE called a PHRASE.

Country Gardens

Optional Teacher Accompaniment

English Folk Tune
Arr. Randall Hartsell

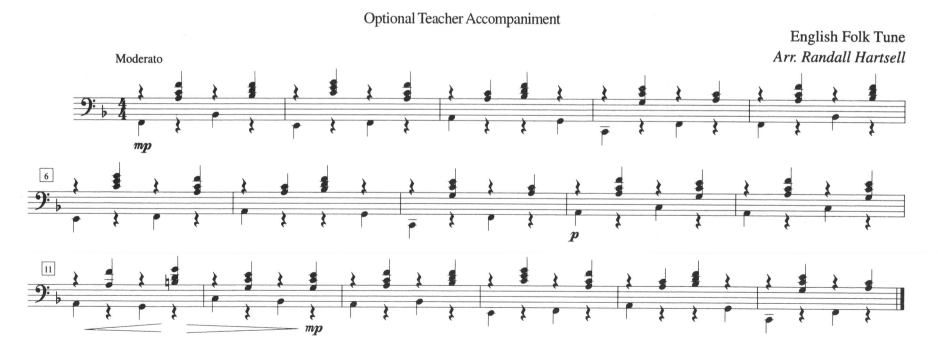

Country Gardens

Play both hands one octave higher when performing as a duet.

English Folk Tune
Arr. Randall Hartsell

Student Position
One Octave Higher When Performing as a Duet

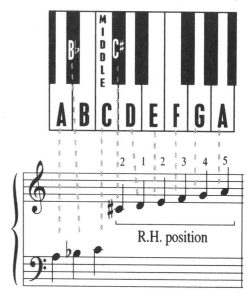

Dynamics

DYNAMICS are suggestions made by the composer to help create contrasts in your music. Watch for the *mf* in this piece. It means mezzo forte or medium loud. The *mp* means mezzo piano or medium soft.

Turkish March
(from *The Ruins of Athens*)

Optional Teacher Accompaniment

Ludwig van Beethoven
Arr. Randall Hartsell

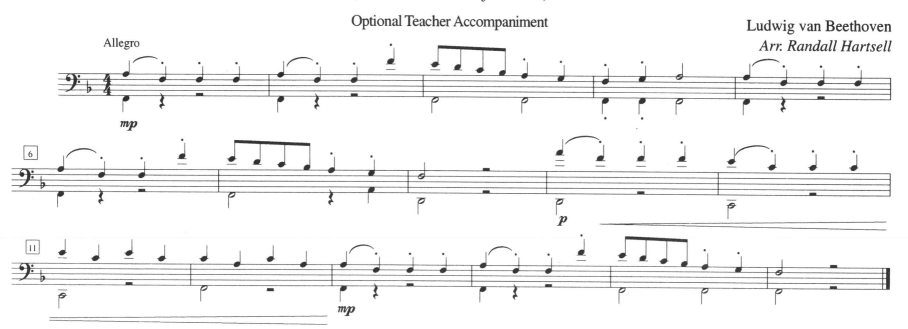

Turkish March

(from *The Ruins of Athens*)

Play both hands one octave higher when performing as a duet.

Ludwig van Beethoven
Arr. Randall Hartsell

TEACHING LITTLE FINGERS TO PLAY

TEACHING LITTLE FINGERS TO PLAY

by John Thompson

A series for the early beginner combining rote and note approach. The melodies are written with careful thought and are kept as simple as possible, yet they are refreshingly delightful. All the music lies within the grasp of the child's small hands.

00412076 Book only $6.99
00406523 Book/Audio...$9.99

TEACHING LITTLE FINGERS TO PLAY ENSEMBLE

by John Thompson

A book of intermediate-level accompaniments for use in the teacher's studio or at home. Two possible accompaniments are included for each *Teaching Little Fingers* piece: a Secondo or Primo part, as well as a second piano part for studios that have two pianos/keyboards.

00412228 Book only $5.99

DISNEY TUNES

arr. Glenda Austin

10 delightful Disney songs: The Bare Necessities • Can You Feel the Love Tonight • Candle on the Water • God Help the Outcasts • Kiss the Girl • Mickey Mouse March • The Siamese Cat Song • Winnie the Pooh • You'll Be in My Heart (Pop Version) • Zip-A-Dee-Doo-Dah.

00416748 Book only $9.99
00416749 Book/Audio...$12.99

CHRISTMAS CAROLS

arr. Carolyn Miller

12 piano solos: Angels We Have Heard on High • Deck the Hall • The First Noel • Hark! The Herald Angels Sing • Jingle Bells • Jolly Old Saint Nicholas • Joy to the World! • O Come, All Ye Faithful • O Come Little Children • Silent Night • Up on the Housetop • We Three Kings of Orient Are.

00406391 Book only $6.99
00406722 Book/Audio...$10.99

CLASSICS

arr. Randall Hartsell

11 piano classics: Bridal Chorus (from *Lohengrin*) (Wagner) • Can-Can (from *Orpheus in the Underworld*) (Offenbach) • Country Gardens (English Folk Tune) • A Little Night Music (from *Eine kleine Nachtmusik*) (Mozart) • Lullaby (Brahms) • Ode to Joy (from Symphony No. 9) (Beethoven) • Symphony No. 5 (Second Movement) (Tchaikovsky) • and more.

00406550 Book only $6.99
00406736 Book/Audio...$10.99

HYMNS

arr. Mary K. Sallee

11 hymns: Amazing Grace • Faith of Our Fathers • For the Beauty of the Earth • Holy, Holy, Holy • Jesus Loves Me • Jesus Loves the Little Children • Joyful, Joyful, We Adore Thee • Kum Bah Yah • Praise Him, All Ye Little Children • We Are Climbing Jacob's Ladder • What a Friend We Have in Jesus.

00406413 Book only $6.99
00406731 Book/Audio...$10.99

TEACHING LITTLE FINGERS TO PLAY MORE

by Leigh Kaplan

Teaching Little Fingers to Play More is a fun-filled and colorfully illustrated follow-up book to *Teaching Little Fingers to Play*. This book strengthens skills learned while easing the transition into John Thompson's *Modern Course, Book One*.

00406137 Book only $6.99
00406527 Book/Audio...$9.99

MORE DISNEY TUNES

arr. Glenda Austin

9 songs, including: Circle of Life • Colors of the Wind • A Dream Is a Wish Your Heart Makes • A Spoonful of Sugar • Under the Sea • A Whole New World • and more.

00416750 Book only $9.99
00416751 Book/Audio...$12.99

MORE EASY DUETS

arr. Carolyn Miller

9 more fun duets arranged for 1 piano, 4 hands: A Bicycle Built for Two (Daisy Bell) • Blow the Man Down • Chopsticks • Do Your Ears Hang Low? • I've Been Working on the Railroad • The Man on the Flying Trapeze • Short'nin' Bread • Skip to My Lou • The Yellow Rose of Texas.

00416832 Book only $6.99
00416833 Book/Audio...$10.99

MORE BROADWAY SONGS

arr. Carolyn Miller

10 more fantastic Broadway favorites arranged for a young performer, including: Castle on a Cloud • Climb Ev'ry Mountain • Gary, Indiana • In My Own Little Corner • It's the Hard-Knock Life • Memory • Oh, What a Beautiful Mornin' • Sunrise, Sunset • Think of Me • Where Is Love?

00416928 Book only $6.99
00416929 Book/Audio...$12.99

MORE CHILDREN'S SONGS

arr. by Carolyn Miller

10 songs: The Candy Man • Do-Re-Mi • I'm Popeye the Sailor Man • It's a Small World • Linus and Lucy • The Muppet Show Theme • My Favorite Things • Sesame Street Theme • Supercalifragilisticexpialidocious • Tomorrow.

00416810 Book only $6.99
00416811 Book/Audio...$12.99

EXCLUSIVELY DISTRIBUTED BY

HAL•LEONARD®
CORPORATION
7777 W. BLUEMOUND RD. P.O. BOX 13819
MILWAUKEE, WISCONSIN 53213

All arrangements come with optional teacher accompaniments.

Prices, contents, and availability subject to change without notice.
Disney characters and artwork © Disney Enterprises, Inc.

FOR A COMPLETE SERIES LISTING, VISIT WWW.HALLEONARD.COM

0617